I0630182

Seasons at Shiregreene

Gillian Richardson

Published by G M Richardson, 2023.

SEASONS AT SHIREGREENE

First edition. July 28, 2023.

Copyright © 2023 Gillian Richardson.

ISBN: 978-1777287245

Written by Gillian Richardson.

Table of Contents

Remembering Tobias of Loch Fyne, who tuned our senses to nature

Preface

In the early 1980s, I began this seasonal journal to remember a special place and its role at a formative time in my life. Shiregreene was the second home of our married life after moving to Prince Edward Island, but the first, and only, house we would build. It was my chance to live in the countryside, not quite on a farm, but surrounded by them. All that space, a blank canvas on which to create a garden, fields to explore with country lanes to ramble down and discover the natural world, dark quiet nights with all the stargazing one could wish for, a private sanctuary. The small square of property—about two and a half acres—was the former site of an old homestead on a rural road halfway between the city and the north shore beaches. It wasn't far either way, an easy drive to work, but most weekends Trevor and I chose to stay home and enjoy our 'country estate'. Those stormy winter days when we couldn't venture out on the roads became time treasures to cherish.

Change is constant, though. We didn't expect to leave this acreage after only a couple of years, our rural dreams put on hold. The project was unfinished, so many ideas not fully formed and plans never realized. The job situation called us away and we went west, first to a prairie city and then on to a rural subdivision in a mountain valley. I've spent much of the intervening forty years writing—mostly children's stories—but I recently came upon these essays once again and decided to give the collection a new life as I near the next stage in my own. Perhaps it's because our present home will likely be the last one outside of town for us, as seniors. Once the garden hobby becomes a chore, it will be time to relinquish our little patch of land and find a smaller, suitable space for slower times.

Meantime, I invite you to meander through my memories and share the discoveries of my 20-something self. Reviewing them now, I see a naivete about so much, understandable maybe in those early adult years. It was a starting point, though, since these observations inspired many years of

1

nature study for me, and more than a few blossomed into short stories, picture books and novel scenes. I wouldn't have missed this time and this place for anything.

Introduction

The house arrived in late fall, just before the first snow. It was a prebuilt home, its four parts constructed in a warehouse and then assembled into a side-split design on the prepared foundation. It was ready to live in by mid-December. The construction process churned up the grounds and left us sitting amid a patch of sticky, red Prince Edward Island mud. We were already acquainted with its tenacious personality, having lived several years on the Island. It clung to the tires on the car. It tugged at our boots (wellies, to us) and tried, sometimes successfully, to suck them right off our feet as we slogged up the lane. Turned our golden retriever's legs rusty red, too. Nothing to be done outside now; snow would hide the scars until spring. Then we could begin to put things right again.

The house smelled new, a mixture of paint, varnish and the glue that was used to stick down the linoleum. Even the Franklin stove smelled like hot metal the first few times it was lit. We would be snug and warm as we set to work to turn our house into a home, hanging curtains and pictures, spreading out those favourite possessions that make a place familiar.

That first night, when I switched off the last light, I was struck by the blackness. The dark was not semi-dark like the lamp-lit canyons that are city streets at night, that light that sneaks in around the edges of the curtains or blinds. Most nights, this was can't-see-your-hands-in-front-of-your-face dark. Our only street light was to be the moon beaming in upon our pillows (no need to draw the curtains at the back of the house), or when her soft illumination reflected off the winter landscape.

Along with the dark, it was quiet, hushed, peaceful. Occasionally, I heard the soft swish of a car passing on the country road. An impersonal sound, much like the sighing of the wind, it was not enough to disturb my sleep. When spring came and we were at last able to have the windows open all night, I would be lulled to sleep by a chorus of frogs and spring peepers from the marsh across the road. Later, it would be the crickets' turn. Our wake up call each summer morning would come from a robin singing 'cheerily' even before the first rays of dawn reached Shiregreene.

What had led us to this place? We were essentially city folks who knew little of farming, and after all, wasn't that what country living meant? Looking back, I'm sure it had something to do with the small size of the Island. Only a few minutes drive from the capital city was that ubiquitous place—the countryside. The city itself reminded us more of the small towns of other parts of the country that we knew. So why not? Here was our big chance—country living, with all the conveniences we were used to and only a dozen miles, uncrowded and scenic, to commute to work and shopping. The same distance in another direction took us to the warm, sandy beaches. It promised the best of both worlds.

A desire to be closer to nature was seeping into my consciousness. The Island's weather and seasons exerted a far more powerful influence over our lifestyle than I'd known elsewhere. I was drawn to learn more, feel more, understand more. We had recently become the proud first-time 'parents' to a golden retriever, and shall ever afterwards credit Toby for luring us to explore the intrigues of the out-of-doors.

We planned Shiregreene with all this in mind, positioning the windows of the house to take full advantage of the panorama spread before us. The large front panes in the living room faced east, and overlooked next summer's expanse of grass stretching down a gentle slope to the road, not quite 200 feet away. Beyond that, a herd of black and white cows grazed and wandered from May to November. The maples in the woodlot at the far end of the pasture glowed red and gold as the first signals of approaching autumn. And the setting sun reflected from the windows of houses several miles away on the next hill.

From the kitchen window at the back, we could watch robins that sang among the apple blossoms in what remained of an old orchard. The big birch and majestic fir trees which marked the northwest corner of Shiregreene kept the cold winds at bay. Beyond all these trees, we watched several acres of grain grow tall and golden, and often enjoyed the blazing red-orange sunset through the stark silhouette of the western tree line.

We had chosen a south window in the dining room, to look out upon lawn and flower garden. We welcomed the winter sunbeams that slanted across the rug. As well, it was a place to watch snowshoe hares emerge from the thick growth of evergreens next door. Nestled among the greenery there, only the tip of a chimney visible from here, was the rustic home of our closest neighbours.

SEASONS AT SHIREGREENE

Near the dining room corner, a huge, old snowball bush which we had taken great care not to disturb during construction of the house, bloomed with enormous white pompoms in June. All year round it was a home and way-station for a host of feathered visitors. Our bush was a symbol of permanence and stability, we learned, being the mother to an unknown number of others, separated and replanted at farm homes along the road.

Perhaps there is now no need to explain why we christened our home 'Shiregreene'. It may have been our English ancestry that suggested naming it at all. Certainly we hoped to find all kinds of the things that are 'nature', from the rainbow collection of lupines growing wild along the roadside, from the wild roses popping up everywhere in the lawn, to tiny, darting hummingbirds, snakes in the old well and maybe even 'hobbits' if one looked hard enough. Our new home graciously revealed its charm to us and became a friend, part of the family. It was our first home in the country and we were yet unaware that our hearts would never leave it.

GILLIAN RICHARDSON

Part I: White Fields and Wind Drifts
Track Tales

Beyond the old apple orchard and the big birch that guarded the northwest boundary of Shiregreene, a world of intrigue, drama, tragedy and delight enticed us. A never-ending series of tales lay written on the winter snow for anyone who'd take the time to read them.

The crisp, mid-winter Saturday morning air set my blood pumping as I boldly tramped a line of snowshoe tracks, following the dog across the middle of the open field. Beneath the glistening carpet, fresh and thick, lay the red-brown furrows left from the fall tilling that awaited the seeds for next summer's grain crop. I stopped, out of breath, at the ragged line of birch, poplar and beech trees that divided this field from the next, and turned to look back at the trail I had left.

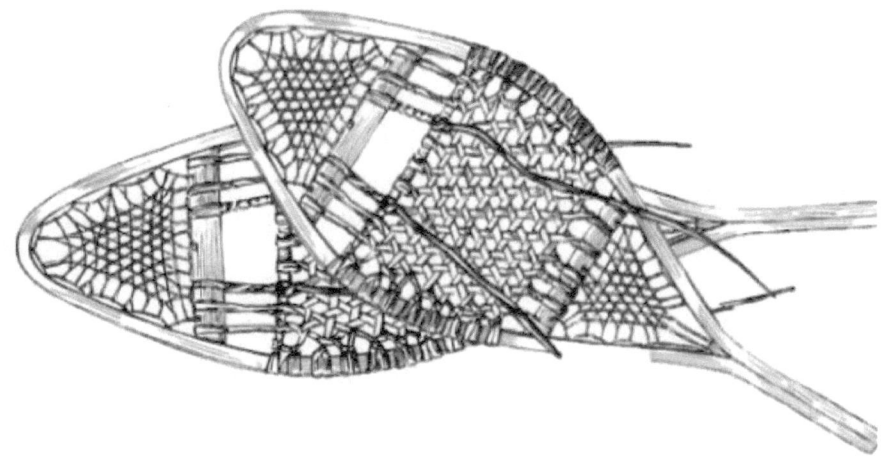

Huge, oval dents now marred the otherwise clean expanse, as if some extra-planetary alien had visited. Was I the only brave pioneer to tread there? Would others follow now that I had broken the trail? And what had I seen in my haste? Not a sign of life, except for my dog's waving tail as he bounded ahead. I'd only heard the swish-swish of my snowshoes, and my own puffs of breath. The exercise worked to clear my mind of a week's worth of nine to five routine. Good for me. But from the point of view of the timid hare or the tiny meadow vole, I had done a foolish thing. Taking short cuts often led the inexperienced to a premature demise. Those who lived to see another day had learned it was far more prudent to travel the edges, even though it might take considerably more time—which then became the reward of the cautious. Ignoring the message proclaimed by that blank space—*nothing to see here, move along*—was one of the ways we humans set ourselves at odds with the rules of nature. We like to proclaim our presence rather than conceal it. Maybe I should remember I was actually a visitor in someone else's domain.

Sobered by these thoughts, I pondered my next move. Hopefully it would be more subtle. I glanced to my left where our closest neighbour's land, a quarter section largely of fir trees, fell gently downhill away from our road. This tract of land remained mostly untouched, as my neighbours liked to encourage close communion with nature. To my right, the tree line thickened to become a small mixed woodlot, a windbreak left between the fields. I chose this direction to begin my search.

Barely a half dozen steps along the edge of the woods, I found my first treasure of the day—tracks left by a snowshoe hare. Plentiful all over the Island, hares provide the red fox, several species of birds of prey and the two-legged variety of hunter with unlimited prey. I saw the hare in my mind, its oversized hind feet reaching with each leap to land ahead of the smaller fore-paws, the graceful motion carrying it easily over the deepest snow. The story of its print pattern is one of the easiest to read—if the space between each cluster is large, or if it zigged and zagged, chances are it sensed danger. When the snow is trampled by many prints, and dotted with numerous dark round droppings, likely it stopped to reach up and nibble the tender twigs accessible from the higher elevation of the drifts. At home, our apple trees have been neatly pruned all around by browsing bunnies.

Even though these tracks are so familiar that some might dismiss them as uninteresting, there is always a story to tease one's imagination. This hare had not been using its stare-of-the-art snowshoes for flight. Its tracks were too close together. Perhaps it was just out for a moonlight hop, relying on its cleverly designed camouflage while it scrounged for edibles. It could be there even now, standing like a porcelain statue, watching my every move. Unless it flicked a black-tipped ear or twitched its nose, it could be invisible in plain sight. More likely, it had found a sheltered place at dawn among the dense evergreens to spend the more dangerous daylight hours resting or tidying its winter wardrobe. An Island hare is luckier than its cousins in the Arctic or the open prairie where there is little shelter. This hare would rarely need to carve out a form or depression in the open, to huddle with legs pulled in close and ears lowered onto its back, another hump in the snow for the wind to sweep across. Whatever their habitat, Nature has bestowed upon hares a wealth of protective devices—keen ears, sensitive nose, a coat to match the landscape in any season, fleet feet. But then it's only fair, when so many are out to make a meal of them!

I continued alongside the trail of my invisible companion until another plot sketched in snow distracted me. These tracks were similar, though quite a bit smaller than those of my friend the hare. From the base of one tree, they led me to another, then on to the next. A red squirrel had been here, roused from its half-sleep by a spell of mild weather, or gnawing hunger pangs.

The squirrel is not a true hibernator, since it will emerge from its cozy nest in a tree cavity a number of times throughout the winter. Those hours spent last fall hiding seeds and cones, mushrooms and berries, now provide cold weather snacking. Bits of fir cone littering the snow betray the location of such a food cache. The red squirrel is one creature who believes in making hay while the sun shines—and reaps its rewards later.

Here among the trees I found evidence of another winter wanderer. This time I almost need a magnifying glass to see the detail of the precise little prints with the drag-mark of a tail in between. But as soon as they vanish into a perfectly round hole in the snow, there is no doubt. No heavyweight made these tracks. Yet the diminutive meadow mouse has strength enough to bulldoze, in mole fashion, a maze of tunnels through the snow. There, it can travel in relative safety as long as the snow stays deep and soft.

On this day the snow that had accumulated within the confines of the woodlot was perfect for both mice and snowshoers. Here, the wind had been unable to hurl its full force at the drifts, pounding them to rock hard mounds as it will in exposed places. My snowshoes sank several inches into the fluff, making a satisfying scrunch. It was not nearly loud enough, however, to hide the presence of a woodpecker—probably a hairy or smaller downy—somewhere up ahead. The staccato hammering echoed sharply through the bare branches.

Emerging on the far side of the woods, I encountered yet another track. A single line of rounded marks marked the passage of a crafty fox. It had accurately placed its hind feet exactly in the holes left by its front ones, giving the impression it could have walked on two feet. This neat, dotted line stretched across the field ahead like stitches on a wintry quilt.

So... someone else did cross open spaces—though probably not in broad daylight! Mind you, the fox, being the largest wild mammal on the Island (until the early 80s, when coyotes arrived) has few enemies other than humans. I left my beaver-tail snowshoe prints alongside its own, wondering what the fox would make of them if it passed this way tonight. Its trail turned to wend its way along the next hedgerow. There it made a few detours, to push a highly inquisitive nose into a mouse hole or two. The fox is a clever, economical hunter—it wouldn't waste time or energy digging unless the scent was fresh. It knows the habits of its prey very well. And those mice, probably motionless far below, listened until their old enemy went on its way.

Farther on, a peculiar design on the snow's surface took my attention. Two fan-shaped depressions and the end of a trail of tiny rodent prints told the story as well as words on a page. A bird of prey had skimmed low over the ground and caught a careless mouse. Slowing its flight, it snatched the small morsel with outstretched talons. Its huge wings had dipped so deeply that the tips had brushed the snow and left finger-like shapes printed there. It could have been a snowy owl, that ghostly wraith that haunts the frozen darkness over much of southern Canada in mid-winter, or perhaps a great horned owl. No matter, for a small mouse seldom gets a second chance against such a masterful hunter.

As I completed my circle of the hay field, still another pattern in the snow revealed last night's activity. A three-toed mark, clear and crisp, told of a ruffed grouse that had wandered here in search of seeds and dried-up berries. As I watched, the wind began to sift loose snow into it, wiping the slate clean again.

The owners of these tracks were not far away, the night shift probably tucked up somewhere to sleep away the daylight hours. At sundown, they would cautiously emerge to take up their endless search for food. But thanks to the new snow I'd seen them all, snooped into their business and learned some of their secrets—without actually running across a single creature in the flesh. Now, my tracks added another tale to be read by anyone who should chance to pass by.

A Secret Place

We came upon it quite by accident—which is exactly the way it had come to be there. At once it became a special place, our secret.

The bright, crisp day followed a dull, overcast week punctuated by frequent snowfalls and high winds. We often ventured out briefly on bad weather days too, but when the sun broke through, the spirits soared and we found energy to burn. So, that day, my dog and I found ourselves deep in the neighbour's woodlot where we discovered the secret place.

A circle of towering fir trees, already heavy with a soft, white blanket, had stopped much more loose snow from blowing away. They enclosed a sheltered spot, well below the level of the snow banks that surrounded it—a perfect, miniature, walled kingdom. Approaching it, you found yourself looking down from halfway up the trees, the snow reached that high!

Imagining what it felt like to be inside was not enough. I sat back on the tails of my snowshoes and let myself slip over the edge. The soft landing left me struggling to get up. I wondered how the dog would manage the entrance as I watched him peering cautiously at my dilemma from above. Vertical once more, I urged him to come and with no further hesitation, he took the plunge. Part of the embankment began to crumble away beneath him as he half-jumped, half-slid out of control into the abyss. Down he came head first to plop in a heap beside me. Up came a stranger in a white beard and bushy eyebrows. When he shook himself, a small blizzard arose, then settled all around.

We were sheltered from the wind, hidden from anyone passing by outside who didn't realize the woods had a 'downstairs' now. The shadowy tree wells under the skirts of the fir trees made extra little rooms, each opening off the central courtyard where we sat. At once we knew we were not the first visitors after all. Tracks of snowshoe hares led in and out of each room. They had chosen our secret place to gambol in the moonlight last night, unseen by those who sought them in a deadlier game. Maybe it had been their secret too, for at the first sound of an approaching fox, or the ominous shadow of an owl, they could dive for cover to be lost instantly among the network of paths beneath the evergreens.

The dog investigated each trail, sometimes disappearing into the room except for his waving plume of tail. It was intriguing to imagine what lay beyond—could one room hide the tunnel leading to Alice's Wonderland? I settled back to enjoy the meager warmth of the winter sun. A troop of black-capped chickadees flitted in to land on a snow-laden branch. Clumps of the wet stuff plopped down on the dog's back, bringing him shuffling out backwards to see who had caused the disturbance. The fussy, feathery puffs scolded cheekily and flew off to a higher perch in case of retaliation. I decided this would be a good place to hang some chunks of suet, or scatter wild bird seed.

We would try to return often, as long as this special place existed. Who knew how long that might be? It may never have been here before, in exactly this way, and may never be again. If it were not such a short-lived miracle of nature, would it seem so special? Was the attraction the very knowledge that it would change, at the mercy of the wind, sun and snow which are at once capricious and symbols of constancy? We take for granted the old and familiar whenever we venture into the outdoors, while at the same time what we see is always being renewed. Never empty space, place without purpose. Everything waits to be transformed, to evolve. Change is certain. Occasionally, when we stop to see, not merely to look, we are lucky enough to witness a brief, precious moment of existence.

Too soon, the sun slipped behind the tall firs, plunging the courtyard into shadow. It was time to leave, time to return custody of this hidden sanctuary to the forest creatures. From atop the snow bank wall, I hesitated, looking back. I wanted to memorize every detail before Toby and I trudged home. It would be hard not to share this bit of magic. But having entrusted us with her secret, did Nature know that only one of us would never be tempted to tell?

Visitors to the Big Birch

It was one of those terribly "blustery days" as Winnie the Pooh might say. The wind had steadily increased as the afternoon wore on. Riding in from the west, on the back of the wind, the clouds appeared small and scattered at first but soon multiplied and organized as if their sole purpose was to blot out the blue sky altogether. Now nearly dusk, details became hazy and shadowy places materialized. The clouds had thickened to a solid-looking mat suggesting yet another imminent snow storm. Already a deep blanket covered the ground. The restless snow spirits, constantly on the move, hissed and sighed as they drifted like puffs of dry ice on a stage set.

Watching the gathering gloom from the kitchen window as I made supper, I was thankful for the umpteenth time for our windbreak. Some thoughtful pioneer whose homestead this had been years ago, had planted or left undisturbed the spruce, now tall and thick. The big birch clump had thrived too, occupying a high point at the northwest corner, a huge crown towering over its main trunk. Tonight, it swayed and moaned before the gusty wind like a tortured giant. Nothing was at peace out there, as the wind jostled all the naked trees and bushes.

SEASONS AT SHIREGREENE

But suddenly a more distinct shape caught my eye, a definite, darker patch among the blur of moving branches. It seemed to cling precariously amid the birch twigs, thrust back and forth, rocking in the breeze. Was there really something there, or was it just the shadows playing tricks? And then a second dark blob joined it, seeming to rise up from the ground. As I watched, completely captivated by now, both ghostly shapes began to move about in the tree. Only when a particularly strong gust of wind bowed the whole tree forward did the shapes take on a recognizable form. They spread their wings to keep their balance and rode the branches like a storm-tossed ship.

Supper was in danger of being very well done, but I reached for the binoculars anyway. In the fast fading light I could make out the pair of ruffed grouse that had come to feed on tender birch buds, one of their favourite foods. The hunger that drove them to brave the wind must have been much stronger than caution. I watched them ride the swirling sea until it was too dark to pick them out anymore.

Next morning, evidence of the visitors lay scattered on the ground. Plenty of three-toed footprints covered a trampled patch of snow close to the trunk. Of course, it had all been a clever plan. The birds had not been in danger in the swaying branches at all. They'd used the wind to knock down more buds so they could feed on the ground where they were more at home. But it was the first time I had seen grouse so close to the house. It was likely difficult for them to find other food in the unusually deep snow.

What snow deprives the grouse of in food, though, it can repay in another way. They are able to use deep drifts as shelter if the snow is soft, by simply diving into them and snuggling down for the night. Nothing is without risk, however. Should freezing rain catch the birds already buried, they would become prisoners under an icy topping which could be impossible to penetrate.

Now that they had discovered a source of food it was the first of many visits this pair of grouse would make to the big birch. Another evening, much earlier so there was still ample light to see by, I noticed the smaller of the pair was using only one leg. The other dangled uselessly at an odd angle. Even so, she was able to balance satisfactorily in the branches with the aid of her wings. The injury did nothing to deter her from feeding on branches far up the tree close to her mate. Later in the winter, only the male came to the feeding spot. His lady's handicap may have proven more of a disadvantage on the ground where a hungry red fox perhaps fulfilled his role in nature's scheme.

During the remaining weeks of winter, our birch revealed some of the many services it had been providing over the years. Other birds and small woodland creatures also knew the big tree as a hospitable place in the frozen land. By day, tiny chickadees and sparrows came to pick among the scraps knocked to the ground by wind or grouse. Bluejays and juncos searched through the litter for a snack. Mice left their tracks at night. A whole community of nature relied on the huge tree. For us, it provided shelter, a source of delight by its sheer size (how old was it?) and elegant bearing, and on especially cold evenings, logs cut from a large broken branch crackled comfortingly in our wood stove.

Storm Warming

The first signs may not necessarily be visible ones. Often it's more a feeling, a strange expectancy, a sensation of knowing a big storm is coming.

Seeking something more tangible, you watch the sky, looking to the west for the first warnings. With an uncertain anxiety, you see a silent grey, cloud cover has begun to reach out, dragging its shadow across the land. Nothing too ominous yet.

Soon the wind stirs, teasing, testing, not yet threatening. The first scattering of snow flakes begins to drift aimlessly about. They seem to irritate the intermittent wind, until the flurries increase in earnest, getting caught on the edges of things. Settle into the corners of window frames. Little mounded caps grow on fence posts, coat rural mailboxes and stop signs. Gradually a billowy white comforter snuggles down over the countryside.

The wind grows bolder, and begins to swirl the snow into miniature cyclones. Now a sense of urgency settles in. Ever larger drifts collect against walls and hedgerows. The weather has closed down upon the Island, the wind-driven snow obscuring everything. Passing traffic glides in silence, headlight eyes peering through the whiteout. Windshield wipers dash the clinging flakes from the glass in a futile attempt to improve vision.

GILLIAN RICHARDSON

Thicker and heavier snow tumbles. Hollows fill in, the rolling landscape becomes deceptively smooth and even. It is only early afternoon but many rural-dwelling Islanders are already heading home. They've seen it happen many times—get stuck in town now, and it may be days before you get home. They know too well what the wind will do to all that is familiar. Soon previous snowplow cuts will have drifted in. Mailboxes which stood proudly on their posts, surrounded by bright petunias in summer to mark the entrance to their owners' lane, quickly disappear in the wake of the snowplow's blade. Normal routines must surrender to the wind now. Until it releases its grip, things will remain at a standstill—no snowplows, no school buses, no milk trucks and no mail delivery. Everything waits. Everything is put on hold.

On such occasions, if the snow is a good consistency, we find it hard to resist strapping on our snowshoes and going for a walk. It is an emotional as well as physical challenge. The wind and snow assault us from all directions. Sometimes we reach the nearby shelter of our neighbour's woods out of breath, with legs feeling weak from the exertion. If we feel diminished, intimidated by the awesome power of nature, at the same time we sense a resurgence of inner strength, snug inside our wind-proof suits. We've braved the fury instead of cowering indoors. We are not completely at its mercy. We've had a chance to know the forces present there, to meet them on their own terms with only the aid of snowshoes to help us move about. Afterwards, a steaming cup of hot chocolate has a special taste, like the satisfaction of a well-earned reward.

By suppertime, curtains have been drawn tightly against the dark. Indoors it is cheery, warm and secure. We can almost ignore the sound of the wind whistling around the corners of the house. We don't have to think about the snowflakes that are getting fatter and sloppier. We probably won't notice the shift in the wind either, or realize that the temperature is rising slowly. Not until the icy pellets of freezing rain being to rattle against the front window are we aware of the cruel trick nature is playing. If the temperature drops again overnight, as it usually does, the world will be encased in layers of ice, impossible to snowshoe on, impossible for animals to burrow into, impossible to shovel.

Still to come is the final blow as if to confirm our fears—the lights begin to flicker. The wind is having a tug-of-war with ice-coated power lines. Then, the house is plunged into darkness. Suddenly we miss the refrigerator's hum, the comforting rush of warmth from the furnace, all those cozy noises we weren't even conscious of until they stopped. Somewhere in the tempestuous night, the weight of ice and the force of the wind have combined to bring the cables down. On lonely stretches of highway, miles from town, the poles fall like dominoes. It may be many hours, perhaps days, before the pulse of electricity we depend on is restored.

What to do now? How can life go on without lights, heat, television? And here, we even are without water—the electric pump to our well is useless. It reminds us of the first power failure, when we were newcomers to Island winters, which caught us ill-prepared. But like everyone 'from away', we quickly mended our ways. This time calm prevails. We have learned to improvise.

The box containing odds and ends of candles, and matches, is close at hand under the kitchen sink. Stored in the basement, two hurricane laps stand filled and ready. The wood box is full; we'll light the Franklin and soon its heat will drift to the rooms upstairs. We had let our instincts take charge this time, having filled buckets and kettles with water hours ago. High winds and heavy snow warning, the radio had said. It's a common pastime to doubt the weatherman, but better safe than sorry in winter-time. We even filled the bathtub with enough water to keep the toilet tank topped up—one of the comforts of life we refuse to be bullied out of by a mere snowstorm. For a long siege, the kitchen cupboards are well stocked and summer's lobster-cooking pot sits on top of the wood stove, already turning snow to hot water. The pioneer spirit must lie dormant in all of us to be stirred awake when we are reduced to the basics. Is that why scrambled eggs taste so superb cooked on the propane camp stove on the kitchen counter?

There remains only the problem of keeping occupied. The flickering candle light does not seem strong enough for reading, though in times past it was more than adequate. With nothing more pressing to do than wait for the snow-water to boil, there's actually time to think! The Island countryside in winter is no place for those who fuss and fume over delays, work piling up at the office, cancellations. We found it surprisingly easy to adopt this secret of the lifestyle here. No need to feel helpless simply because we couldn't get out, or anyone else get in. It was like an unburdening of daily cares and responsibilities for a while, with absolutely no guilt attached. It was no fault of ours, after all. Nature had taken charge, the weather was absolute master now. Perhaps she knows what is best for us from time to time. Soon enough, the world would be able to get at us again.

Years later, when we entertained neighbours in another part of the country with only slightly exaggerated tales of the hardships of Island winters, the reaction was one of horror. How did you stand it? What did you do? How could anyone cope with being snowbound, cut off from everything for days? You must have been glad to leave. All agreed it was strange to enjoy living in such a place. Inwardly—and outwardly—we laughed.

By the mere telling of the tales, all the memories came flooding back. How we missed it! How much richer we felt for the experience! I was immeasurably glad we had been there, and sorry they might never know the special feelings those memories brought. I wondered what occasions they found amid the daily turmoil of city life to stop for a breathing space, to take time to reflect, to stand back and watch themselves go by. Despite all the sound and fury those Island winter storms could muster, the predominant sense, for us, was of peace.

The Circle Game

Our golden retriever, Toby, always enjoyed a romp in the woods and fields that surrounded Shiregreene. With endless trails to follow, occasionally his diligence was rewarded when a snowshoe hare or covey of grey partridge would burst forth from nowhere and he could give chase. His sharp ears could pick out the tiniest rustlings amid the tangle of bushes in the woods. I had simply to watch the dog to know if anything was about. His body language told me the direction and whether the subject in question was something to be confronted or merely a curiosity. And if his eyes and ears could not detect any living presence, his keen nose told him who had passed this way recently. The scent trails led him a merry chase as he read and explored each and every one. Since he ran ten miles to my one, he always got plenty of exercise.

On this particular day in late winter, the sun felt stronger, its warmth making me feel drowsy and over-dressed as I tramped along the edge of the neighbours' woods. The dog lagged a short distance behind, having taken one of his many detours. I stopped to unzip my jacket and stuff my mitts into my pockets. A small movement caught my eye. Several yards ahead a hare stood, stretched to its full height to get a better view of us, ears tuned to catch every sound from our direction.

I took a slow step back and leaned carefully against a convenient tree to watch. The hare was in no danger, whether it realized it or not. It would merely get some exercise and a chance to show off the impressive design of its long legs and custom-made snowshoes. I had seen it happen far too often to be worried about the end result. Somehow, Toby never failed to fall for the old zig-zag trick. Perhaps no one ever told him the shortest distance between two points is a straight line. He insisted on following his capable nose, as his ancestry dictated, before bothering to look up.

GILLIAN RICHARDSON

I glanced over my shoulder to see my four-footed companion still sniffing his way up the slight rise I had climbed, his nose as usual glued to some mysterious trail. The hare sensed the approach, but sat motionless, no doubt calculating its getaway. It seemed to have dismissed me as a potential danger. It would soon become apparent it need not concern itself over the dog either! Then, to my initial bewilderment, instead of darting off in the opposite direction, the hare made one large leap, proceeding at an angle towards me. Slowly and deliberately it hopped in a rough circle about twenty yards in diameter, directly in the path of the still unmindful dog. The plan complete, the hare launched itself off with another gigantic leap, to be instantly swallowed up by the trees and shrubs.

Recognition began to dawn in my bemused brain and I settled back to watch the outcome. Still vacuuming old scent trails, my canine friend wandered closer. Suddenly his path crossed the arc of the circle and he was instantly transformed. Oh, to have such a sense of smell! His ears shot up. He quickly scanned the area but of course there was no visible clue. Immediately he set off at a run, nose to the ground, right around the cleverly laid track. The gap left by the hare at its departure point was suitably large. Round and round went the dog, completely foxed—or should it be 'hared'—until at last his rush dwindled to a halt. His look of puzzlement was genuine. He was probably wondering why laughter had me doubled up, leaning on the tree trunk.

As for the perpetrator of the hoax, that was one crafty rabbit, and what a story it would have to tell its children! Surely the temptation to forgo a head start was impossible to resist. I could almost imagine the critter slapping its knee in mirth, watching us from behind a nearby bush.

Part 2: Red Mud and Melodies
Spring Songs

The orchestra of spring presents an exhilarating, multifaceted concert after a long winter of sighing snow and querulous wind. The countryside erupts with musical sounds, a symphony of the new season. The warming sun has the role of conductor, setting the ice and snow dripping, the ditches rushing and the streams gurgling. The trumpeting winds that hooted and howled all winter in fits of temper become balmy breezes that whistle and sigh from the string section. Rain drums on the roof, then trickles, flute-like down the eavestrough and plinks a rhythm from branch tips. The crescendo builds until, one morning, you realize a chorus of voices has been added—the birds have returned.

From April onwards, songbirds on the Island lend their cheery voices to the energetic season. *"We're back, we're back, warm days are ahead,"* they seem to say. Someone must have decreed that only joyful noises may be heard. What is sheer beauty to us, however is serious business to them. Their music festival has a serious purpose, other than entertaining winter-weary humans. Decked out in their finest spring garb, the males of each species rehearse the numbers they will use to attract a mate or defend their chosen territory. The warm season is a short one here. There is no time to waste on frivolities.

In the woods beyond Shiregreene's orchard, my favourite activity was to stand still, eyes closed, and let the birdsong fill my mind. The cheery assortment of whistles, trills and twitters had a restorative quality, an effect much like the gentle spring rain had on the land, a reassurance that the cycle was complete once more; spring had pushed aside the frigid grip of winter. The woods, at last, had come alive again with the melodies of robins, sparrows, warblers and thrushes.

I liked to listen for one special song, though, that will always typify, for me, the Canadian outdoors. The white-throated sparrow with its distinctive black and white striped head and yellow eye patch has a far-reaching voice. Once you have heard "Sweet Canada, Canada, Canada" ring out clear and strong across the treetops, you will understand. It soars above the chorus of other songs and echoes in the rain-soaked woods when the sun breaks through. I would usually hear it before I'd see the songster. Then the trick was to move quietly in the direction of its call. I was always amazed at how far away it might be. Once, I located the dapper little bird immediately beside me in a spruce tree and was treated to a front row seat for a concert as a reward for my diligence.

Those ambitious enough to forsake a cozy bed for a six-thirty AM walk, might be rewarded with the sight and sound of wavering lines of Canada geese strung out across the pale sky. Some will reclaim last spring's local nesting area, while others hurry to keep their appointment on some northern lake. Their vibrant honking lingers on the breeze even when they're only small specks in the distance.

Down by the pond, another common Island resident may be announcing his presence. The scratchy call of the red-winged blackbird seems a perfect tone for those first days when the air feels flush with heat, reminiscent of the drone of cicadas later in the summer. That's when the black male with his distinct red epaulets can be found in any Island marsh distracting attention from his more quietly attractive brown-striped mate. Settled on her nest among the reeds, she seems content to let him be the show-off. As usual, Nature has laid her plans well. Even a small pond, like the one over the hill behind Shiregreene will have its complement of red-wings. Occasionally, black ducks nested there too, like the pair who took off quacking in alarm at the approach of nosy humans and their dog.

The best was yet to come, though, and we'd have to wait until almost the end of May for the repertoire to be complete. Usually we'd listen especially for this fellow, anytime after the middle of the month, hoping he'd be early. But Islanders say his arrival invariably coincides with the long holiday weekend, the 24th of May. Sure enough, right on schedule, the first bubbling yodels spilled over the hay field. The bobolinks were back! Their liquid, burbling song tells their name to the rest of the woodland residents. We'd sit by the pond to watch them swoop and glide above the breeze-riffled grass, in a most impressive show. As attractive to look at as they are to hear, the bobolink is the only male warbler with a black throat and breast and a bright yellow patch on the back of his head. Other species have a darker head and lighter colouring underneath. A favourite sighting for us, the bobolink at one time was considered a pest in the rice growing areas of the southern US during fall migrations. Here, they always dominated the scene upon arrival, bringing the spring return of songbirds to a grand finale.

That first evening of the bobolink's arrival, we lingered longer than usual to enjoy their encores. The last rays of rose-pink light found us trudging up the slope to the gap in the tree line. We passed through and stopped for a moment to glance back at the fiery sunset. At that instant, a lone singer took the stage to entertain, perched high atop a birch tree barely bursting into leaf—a rose-breasted grosbeak. Even in the fading light, its black suit accented with a crimson ascot easily drew our attention. This male would trill his song in this same spot each spring evening. Sometimes confused with the robin's melody, the grosbeak produces a richer tone. After hearing him nightly for a while, I could easily tell the difference. Next spring I'd have to tune my ear all over again.

We crossed the last section of field heading for home just as the farmer's tractor turned off the highway into the lane. We exchanged waves, but our friend didn't stop to chat on this warm still evening. The soil was drying nicely and conditions were ideal. Like the birds, the farmer had no time to waste. He might plough 'til nearly midnight, headlights bobbing along, weaving back and forth across the land.

We turned out the lights and settled under the cozy bedclothes, listening through the first open windows of spring to the steady thrum of the tractor engine. A contrast to the birds' music, still this was an appropriate song to the awakening land, one whose comforting rhythm would lull us to sleep.

Fog

I had just enough time before leaving for work in the city, only a fifteen minute drive, to take the dog for a morning romp. The weather forecast had promised a clear, mild April day. To begin, though, early morning mist hung over the fields. I knew, by noon, the sun would have burned away all traces of it. We set off anyway, seeking some inspiration for the day ahead. We would discover a different source for our pleasure today, however, not in what we saw but in what we did not.

Each footstep left a deep print in the soft wet earth of the ploughed field. Red soil stuck to my wellies, turning them from black to rust and the dog's legs from blond to Irish setter red. We reached the gap in the tree line, cut long ago to allow the passage of tractor and hay baler. Now, it framed the entrance to a world of murky, grey, shadowy nothingness. The valley into which the hay field sloped was filled to the brim with soupy fog.

Normally, I'd be able to see all the way to the next country road, a mile or more away. I'd see how the land rolled gently into the valley, lying nestled between woodlots and pastures. I could trace the course of the small stream that meandered along at the lowest point. That vista of field and woods, pasture and stream stretching west towards the red-roofed farm building on the distant road brought visual rewards through every season.

In spring, the first hint of awakening life appeared as a fine, green fuzz on trees and bushes. By mid-summer, the sloping land was lush and verdant, turning rich gold in fall. Under a silent covering of winter white, the fields rested, waiting. You could almost inhale the peace, the calm, the orderliness that helped to keep the daily confusion of life in perspective.

This morning a filmy curtain had dropped on that familiar stage setting. Not a barrier, forbidding us to enter. Instead, inner knowledge drew us forward, assurance of what lay ahead even without the sense of sight to confirm it. When we rely primarily on visual signals to explain the world around us, much goes unnoticed. When that sense is impaired to any degree, we have a chance to test some other equipment, and in doing so, to perceive the familiar as if new.

The dog bounded off into the woodlot, the sound of his footsteps muffled by the sticky sodden carpet of leaf mould from many autumns. Drips spattered dully from the tips of spring-swollen buds. The air was saturated with the clinging wetness, like an over-loaded sponge. No wind stirred. No bird sang. A grey fog blanket smothered the whole world.

Like a ghostly apparition, the dog sniffed around the base of a nearby tree. I sniffed too. The air hung heavy with the tangy odour of damp soil and rotting vegetation. It was a heady, earthy smell, yet clean and with a vague sweetness. No smoke, no dust, no exhaust fumes.

Chill fingers of clammy dampness touched my cheek. Limp strands of hair poked out beneath my jacket hood. I shivered involuntarily, feeling the grayness snuggle around me.

As we glided along into the void, the curtains closed behind us, instantly obliterating any evidence of our passing. We existed in a sphere, a few feet in diameter, its outward edges changing as we walked. For now. there was no world out there, no stress, no bills, no wars. All we could see was all there was to see. Somehow it felt safe, defined. Enough. The limits were there, but without the loss of a sense of freedom.

We made our way back past looming shadows of fir trees that bordered the hay field, standing like sentinels. As we headed home to greet the work day ahead all senses keen and renewed, I knew we'd heard the world breathing.

Small Discoveries

Spring may be the shortest season on Prince Edward Island and the hardest to grab hold of, but there are rewards for the persistent. It is an impatient, unsettled time, filled with small beginnings and irritating reversals. Considered singly, each event seems of little consequence and you have the impression progress has stalled. But added together, they inevitably become the vague Island transition between barren winter and full-blooming summer.

As the days begin to lengthen, the sun tackles the last, shrinking patches of granular snow. Bit by bit, the first tentative blades of Shiregreene's lawn emerge. Yet the meltwater trapped in hollows of red earth in the flowerbed still films over each night with ice. The evening air still has a sharpness that sends you indoors for a heavier sweater. Cautiously, as if they know it's really too soon, yellowish tips of daffodil spikes appear around the old pump. Tulips are even more prudent—no sign of them yet. But it helps to know the frost is leaving the ground. Spring must be on its way. Just when you've decided to believe in the promise, a late blizzard wipes out all the details with a howling vengeance. Once more the world is a white blank. Now spring will have to start all over again.

Along the south boundary, close up against the neighbour's fir trees, lie old, dirty humps of snow which refuse to melt. The sun never quite reaches that edge and the breeze can still be cool. In among the trees, the snow may last for weeks yet. How can you pinpoint that thing called spring when it's halfway to June, the air is balmy and filled with the humming of insects (those pesky blackflies are back!) and there, under those evergreen boughs...snow?

Even the sun has trouble making up its mind. One day it's warm enough to throw open the windows, shake out the blankets, feel the heat on your face as you sit on the sheltered front step on a Sunday morning. Around back, the rhubarb is well on its way. The buds are plump and ready to pop on every tree. That evening, the mist rolls in and you know it's a whole week's worth. Day after foggy day drags by. You lose track of time; each day looks much like the last. The cold drizzly rain seems endless. Everything drips. These came to be known around Shiregreene as days of 'frizzle and drog' as we would try to make light of another gloomy weather report. The garden would go in late again this year if it didn't dry up in time for the Maylongweekend.

Eventually the last tatty bits of snow melt away, but without the sun to turn things green and make the flowers bloom, there's only red-brown and grey and more red-brown everywhere. There's even a late frost warning if the clouds finally clear out overnight. What price sunshine?

Finally the time will come when we can't wait any longer. We decide to go searching for green. We'll start by exploring the sloppy pasture across the road before the neighbouring farmer brings his small head of dairy cows for the summer. Then the dog would worry the cows. Now, we have it all to ourselves. At the far end, a narrow path leads to the edge of a small stream, gurgling through a patch of scrubby fir trees The bank has been trampled by generations of hooves as their owners stood around in the shade, swishing their tails and chewing sociably. On the moist ground we find what we want—mosses emerging from winter, a fresh green against the dark red-brown soil.

We squelch along the edge of the pasture next, looking for the dainty Mayflower with its cluster of pinkish-white blossoms, or the tiny yellow buttercups that nod in the breeze. A shaft of sun stabs through a hole in the clouds, dazzling us with flashes from the droplets of mist that cling to everything.

This tradition of searching for tangible evidence of spring was born during the waning days of our first winter at Shiregreene. The landscaping plans had been made and remade during the long, dark evenings. We were eager to get started. As soon as the snow began to melt, it laid bare the destruction the building crew had wrought, and it appeared even more devastating than we remembered. The excitement of moving in, followed almost immediately by a pristine covering of snow had softened the impact of the task that lay ahead in the spring. Time has a kind way of diluting the negative images. When at last the bulldozer arrived to give shape to our designs, it remained mired in mud as the rain persisted. The sight of that ugly hulk squatting where I envisaged a clump of fragrant, purple lilacs did nothing to lift the spirits. Even after the clouds finally parted, each day was pronounced 'too wet yet' to finish preparation for the lawn.

Thus began our escapes into the surrounding woods and fields to search for signs of 'greene', for reassurance that time was not standing still. The woodlot behind our home was the perfect environment for the delicate painted trillium. Our initial search turned up a few, but only one in bloom in a patch of bright sunlight; three creamy white petals splashed with a wine coloured blaze. We knew it was unlikely that anyone else would find them. Few people lived near enough to walk there, and the farmer, whose land this was had more important spring chores than looking for flowers. Chances were good that no one would disturb the beauties—and indeed, they bloomed every spring especially for us.

Encouraged by the sun, we would hike down into the gentle valley, all the way to the stream that flowed along at the bottom. Was this part of that other stream, having wended its way underground from the higher land, travelling under the road, beneath Shiregreene's old pump and down through the woods to emerge here? Was it the same water that made the cranberry bog spongy and the wispy tamaracks grow so fast? Here though, the vegetation had not been trodden down. In damp places, fiddleheads would be poking up, small tightly curled fists that stretch out into feathery ferns when the days grow warmer. More small beginnings, more green.

Each spring, our searches led to different discoveries. Once, when we had tramped farther afield than usual, we were delighted to watch brand new foals prancing about on the thick turf, all knobby legs and whisk-broom tails. On another hike along a back lane, lupines spread their whorls of tapering leaves. Soon the delicate shades of purple, pink, blue and white would fill the ditches as the tall flower spikes waved in the breeze to all who passed.

Another day, the dog found the best treasure. After patrolling his 'estate' Toby was sniffing his way back to the house through some rough grass.

Suddenly he did a rapid about-face and pricked up his ears. The tail began to wag furiously, his signal for discovery. We rushed to see, not wanting him to try a mouthful of whatever it was. Huddled among the leaves and grass lay four tiny snowshoe hares, perfect miniatures of the adults. We couldn't leave them there, now that the dog knew of their presence. They were too scared and too small to run so we scooped them up gently and carried them to the edge of the trees. Each warm, throbbing handful barely weighed a few ounces, their brownish-grey fur so soft you could hardly feel it. We tucked them in under the lowest branches, hoping they'd find a safer shelter. We looked around for a parent but none was visible of course. When we looked back, the tiny balls of fluff had vanished too.

We remember when the dog uncovered a nest of naked, newborn field mice, each one an inch of faceless pink. We carefully replaced their comforter of grass, hoping they had not felt a chill. It was impossible to resist one more peek the next day, but the nest was empty. A worried mother had obviously bundled her precious family off to a new spot.

Even after our lawns were thick, the trees and shrubs well established and flowerbeds filled with the promise of bulbs and perennials, we kept up our yearly scavenger hunts. We needed only the sight of something fresh and new, a bit of green or a tiny creature in the first days of life. Then we could really believe in the spring miracle again. Next stop, summer!

Part 3: Sunshine and Special Friends
Humperdink and Other Birds

It can be hard to tell exactly when summer has really taken hold on Prince Edward Island. The cool, windy, wet days of late winter and spring can linger and return to tease us with flurries in late May or even June. Perhaps it is summer when the trees have finally burst into leaf, or when the masses of wildflowers show off their nodding blooms in every uncultivated meadow. Or when my daffodils and tulips hang on long after I felt their time had gone.

Maybe the insects provide the clue. The blackflies and mosquitoes become slightly less insistent. They appear mostly at dawn and dusk, or to remind you that long grass and shady woods should be entered at your own risk. But I think the best clue that summer has truly arrived is a lull, when the first frenzy of bird song has passed and the feathered populace has settled to the serious task of nesting.

We watched the yellow-shafted flickers establish property rights to the old dead trunk over in the southeast corner of Shiregreene. It looked like it had been well used for many summers before we arrived. It was a two-level apartment, but only the penthouse seemed to be occupied this year. The flickers popped in and out and busied themselves hunting for ants over in the orchard, their loud calls of "flicka, flicka, flicka" reverberated among the trees. The black bib and bright flash of white rump darting past gave them away every time despite their speed.

Robins were everywhere in summer. They were usually the first to be heard in the morning and often the last at night. They don't nest very high off the ground, making their sites easy to find. I spotted one nest just about eye level in a bush back in the woods. Although quite accessible, it was well hidden and would have escaped notice had the parents not raised such a fuss at my approach. The male became especially irate, a tactic that usually drives off an intruder. I stole a quick peek, then hurried on my way, out of respect for his efforts.

But I had a dreadful encounter with another robin which unfortunately caused her to abandon a well-planned nest. It rested among the lower boughs of one of the tall firs on the north edge of our land. The bird had chosen the bottom of two close layers of branches, so the top layer formed a natural canopy. I was the cause of her flight, sad to say, but it was entirely unintentional. Having swept up a bag of leaves, grass, dog hair and other accumulated debris from the garage, I took my bag to shake it out under the trees. The plastic crackled, and the bird flew, panic-stricken, almost into my face! I'm not sure which of us was more startled. It took only a moment's search to locate the nest and its three, exquisite blue eggs. I left everything undisturbed for the next few days. But when I checked later, the nest was empty. There hadn't been time for hatching and fledging, so most likely a predator took the eggs. Sorry, robin! Maybe you had time to nest again.

We could only guess the reason for another empty nest that summer, but hoped the story had a happier ending. This one belonged to a ruffed grouse who had chosen a questionable place at the base of a fir tree partway down the edge of a hay field. We thought she was careless to build so close to the open, for the nest really had no protection other than its blend of browns that made it virtually invisible to a casual glance. No doubt she had her reasons, and of course knew better than us. It didn't have the neat precise shape of the robin's nest; rather a collection of dead leaves, grasses, twigs and feathers arranged only enough to contain the beige, mottled eggs.

Toby alerted us to its presence, his nose being one of our best allies. We followed his gaze, but initially saw nothing unusual. Knowing full well that the dog was seldom mistaken, we allowed him to move forward anyway. The grouse decided wisely that the jig was up. She took off with a rush and squawk into the woods. We moved in closer now that we could do no further immediate harm, and marvelled at the camouflage of her nest and its nine eggs.

From higher ground across the field, we kept watch each day through binoculars. The dog was not permitted to go near again. Unlike the robin, though, the grouse did return. She seemed unaware of her observers, occasionally moving her head to enable us to pick her out. In fact, she was probably quite well aware of us. But as long as we did not encroach on the critical distance she had decided on as a safety factor, we were allowed to watch. For almost a week, we did and then one day there was no grouse. After several more days, during which we made sure the bird was absent, our curiosity became too much and an investigation was necessary. The bird and her eggs were gone. We couldn't even find any broken shells and no longer really any shape resembling a nest. Grouse chicks are precocial, so perhaps they had hatched and been hustled away shortly afterwards. Had the red fox we knew hunted these fields caught the grouse family by surprise? We found no clues to solve the mystery.

Upon a special, most welcome visitor to our garden, we bestowed the name of Humperdink. Mistaken momentarily for a large bee, he could be seen frequently hovering before the hanging blooms of the fuchsias I had put in pots on the front step. The ruby-throated hummingbird is attracted to reds and to trumpet-shaped flowers. He also favoured my gladiola and the huge orange-specked lilies in the flower bed.

As he sipped nectar from the blooms, his tiny wings were a blur. I realized I had never actually seen a hummingbird's wings! To do so, I had to catch up with Humperdink one day when he came to rest on a low branch of the snowball bush, only a foot above the snoozing dog's head. The dog's ears twitched slightly at the tiny sound of Humperdink's arrival—a whirr then silence, as the sturdy bits of gossamer were folded along his back. Had the dog looked up, he would have seen only leaves, as the bird became a match for them. From a nearby lawn chair, I marvelled at miniature perching feet and delicate, tapered wings as Humm stretched them.

Hummingbirds make a squeaky chipping sound as they flit among the plants. It's distinctive enough to attract your attention once you realize who's making it. Often, through an open window, I'd hear Humperdink talking to the flowers as he sipped and I could watch him at close range. What a master aviator. As well as hovering, he flew backwards, sideways and pulled rapid disappearing acts that would make a magician blink.

Humm spent many calm, sunny days flitting and 'humming' around the garden. I realized that 'he' was really a 'she', since there was no red patch on her throat. We saw her mate a number of times, so likely they nested somewhere close. Finding the egg-cup sized structure would have been like seeking the proverbial needle and although we watched for it each time we went walking, we were never able to find it. It was enough of a treat that the 'Humms' had chosen our garden for their visits.

Not all of our feathered guests had such peaceful intentions. Not all were able to find a meal waiting passively among the blossoms or crawling on the ground. Most songbirds are prey themselves in the vast food chain, and one avian visitor to our acreage probably instilled dread into many tiny hearts. This was a kestrel, or sparrow hawk.

Though not much bigger than a robin himself, he is swift of wing and quite deadly of beak and talon. I noted his presence one day as I puttered around the garden doing odd chores. Rounding a corner of the house, I barely missed being sideswiped by a close rushing of wings in rapid flight. Alerted as well by a commotion of loud cheeps, I ducked just in time. The escapees were small birds, probably sparrows or chickadees. The pursuer showed me a flash of blue-grey wing, reddish back and black and white facial markings, all in a blur of speed. My bird guide suggested the kestrel and I was later able to confirm this as I watched it hovering over the field behind the house.

From its perch at the top of a tree in the hedgerow, the skilled hunter studied the comings and goings of songsters around my yard. Word spread quickly, however, and the small creatures soon became extra cautious, more adept at travelling unseen as long as the predator was in evidence. Our garden must have been only a small part of its hunting territory, for the kestrel did not remain long. It was seen off and on all that summer. We marvelled at its attractive plumage, its grace and dexterity, but feared for the safety of our other residents whenever it was about.

The presence of birds can easily be taken for granted, if not seen. Their voices are often background 'white noise' in our busy lives. If you stop to imagine how silent the outdoor world would be without them, you suddenly appreciate them as they deserve. They greet each sunrise with their cheery notes, twitter comfortingly after a drenching rain, and close the chapter of each day with a thankful hymn. Having so many opportunities to observe them around Shiregreene ignited a keen interest that I was unaware would grow, and last a lifetime.

No Reason to Fence

Across the road from Shiregreene's sloping front lawn, a dozen young Holstein dairy cows were quartered for the summer months. Their daily schedule of activities consisted of making endless slow circuits of the pasture. On each round, they'd gather for a rest in one corner of the fence nearest the road. A dozen heads would hang over the top strand of wire, blinking huge soulful eyes with lashes any model would envy. A dozen tufted, rope-tails would swish to keep the flies stirred up. Maybe they counted the vehicles passing by. They watched our dog playing on the lawn (also watching them!). By times, they seemed quite interested in trying to figure out what we were up to in the house, since they could look right through our living room window. Then, at some signal obvious only to the cows, they'd all take up their leisurely stroll once again, stopping to graze here and there along the way. At the bottom of the pasture they'd disappear into the trees for a time, or down to the small stream that provided their drinking water. Eventually, they'd reappear, wending their way back up the side fence for another rendezvous in our corner.

Watching the movements of those cows set me to wondering about fences. What purpose did they serve, other than to keep cows moving in never-ending circles, or giving them something to hang their heads over? I began to take more notice of the fences near our land. There were none at Shiregreene. We hadn't had time to decide about fences yet. I could see that Frost's declaration—good fences make good neighbours—was true for us, where the cows were concerned. I preferred to have them watch me from across the road rather than to have them marching through my marigolds. And for the sake of the cows as well as the motorists who were always in a hurry going to or coming from town, it was best to keep them off the road. If the fence succeeded in keeping the cows in, it also served to keep the cars out, a situation of advantage to both parties. Amazingly, a few strands of thin wire provided this mutual security.

However, down the road, an old farmhouse occupied one corner of a section of land. The fields adjacent to it were now leased to someone else to grow grain and potatoes. A white fence, three boards high, neatly partitioned off the acre or two where the house sat. Was it to keep the crops out or the residents in? Doubtless, complaints from either side about trespassing were few. If the purpose was only to mark a boundary, why not a hedge or bushes or trees? No painting required. It might serve as a windbreak, with shade perhaps an added bonus. Birds would be attracted to nest in such edge plantings. But this fence seemed to exist to make a simple statement—this is ours, that is yours. That's all.

Away from the road, in the back fields behind Shiregreene, I often followed a line of irregularly spaced posts—the remains of an old barbed wire fence. It led through open meadows, into thick brush and even at one point across a stream. Among the impenetrable tangle of vegetation, some sections remained intact, although the barbs were ugly with rust. At one break in the line were signs of a path, once well-beaten, but now almost completely over-grown. It wasn't clear to me why this barbed wire fence had been erected in the first place. It marked no obvious boundary. Over the years since it was built, the land must have changed, the forest advancing and the pasture land, if that is what it had been, giving way to a landscape of wildflowers and shrubs. Moisture-loving ferns grew in wild profusion along the stream, sometimes hiding it from view altogether.

Usually, at a point where the fence took a sharp ninety degree turn, I would climb over and cut back across my neighbour's land to Shiregreene. I had never reached a conclusion as to the purpose of this fence until one day I happened to see an unusual bird perched upon a section of the wire near a bush. When I moved closer to try and identify it, the bird flew off before I had chance for more than a brief look. But within the bush, where the wire strand crossed the Y-shaped branch, a compact nest had been woven. The wire formed the perfect anchor for the structure. But for the fence, the nest might not have been built there. But for the fence line that I had followed, it may never had been discovered. From that day, the old barbed-wire fence had a function, at least for me.

If I wandered far enough through the fields past lush rows of potatoes, corn I could barely see over, and acres of fragrant clover, a narrow country land appeared. Many local farmers used these clay roads as a short-cut between highways or to gain access to remote sections of their own land. One farmer kept several ponies in a field along this road, fenced in by the most attractive country style, the split-rail fence. It was my favourite, perhaps because it used natural material that blended in so well with everything around it. The support posts stood at odd angles, forming causal X's. The rails were grey and weathered; no fancy paint job here. Each piece was an individual, hand cut according to the thickness and shape of the wood. Some looked as though they'd just fallen into place rather than being put there by a human hand. That fence had character, not factory precision.

It offered steps at various levels to help in climbing over, but more important, there was always a comfortable spot or two on which to sit. From my perch, I could feed daisies to the ponies who clustered around, glad of some company. Somehow, a split-rail fence seemed the least like a fence. It was friendlier, more approachable, less like a barrier. Whenever I saw a section being used as decoration across a front lawn in town, I was sure those people yearned for country living.

I had one more fence purpose to consider. It might be any kind, since you could barely see it for the hollyhocks or climbing roses planted in front of it. Perhaps it started out as a fence for keeping things in or out, or separating this from that. Once nature took over, however, that purpose no longer seemed to matter. Hollyhocks need something to lean on, morning glories and sweet peas something to climb upon. The fence almost becomes part of the plants, and if its upkeep is neglected, looks perfectly appropriate.

While considering landscape plans for Shiregreene, it was inevitable that the question of fences would come up. But when we were done, there were still no fences. We had no livestock to keep in, nor any wish to keep wildlife out. On both sides of the property, a natural hedgerow of trees and thick undergrowth provided an attractive boundary, a windbreak as well as excellent cover for small birds, snowshoe hares, pheasants, mice and squirrels. No fence could do so much. It kept them always within watching distance.

At the back, we liked the way our land melted into the surrounding fields—most of the time we could imagine we owned it all, as far as the eye could see. No fence interrupted our dream. Our energy went towards planting more trees and lots of bushes that would produce berries to attract the birds. There would be ample places for them nest.

It was hard to resist the idea of building a section of split-rail fence somewhere. But we did. The front would not have been a good choice, for we'd never sit that close to the road anyway. We didn't need to pretend we lived in the country. It's surprising how well hollyhocks will beautify a bare, south-facing wall. The morning glory vines seemed meant to wind their way around the old pump in the front flowerbed. Other wild vines pleased us by turning up where we should have expected them—climbing the old trunk where the flickers nested, or creeping slowly up the apple trees. They looked happiest there, in the places they'd chosen for themselves. And we only had to take a leisurely walk along that clay road to enjoy a split-rail fence.

There may be plenty of reason for fences, but none that we could see were reason enough to build one at Shiregreene.

Tham

Plunk! Splop!

There was water down there alright. But the shaft of the old pump was loose, probably broken part way down the well. Pumping the remaining stub of the handle produced only a weary arm. After dropping in a few pebbles, then listening to guess how far down the water level was, we set to work to seal up the hole. The old iron pump, once the provider of clean, cold well water, was about to become an ornament.

The hexagonal concrete base, almost four feet in diameter, was still intact. We cemented the iron base of the pump shaft securely in place. Then, we fitted a temporary wooden handle, until we could explore the many antique stores and flea markets held all over the Island each summer, and seek out a more authentic replacement.

We had landscaped the front yard with the old pump as its centrepiece. It was to be surrounded by a flowerbed full of bulbs for a spring show of daffodils and tulips, later with brightly coloured geraniums and dahlias. I happily dug and planted, tended to the weeds and kept the edge trimmed for most of the summer before I was even aware that our pump had a tenant.

Tham was a common garter snake, his name being derived from his scientific title, Thamnophis sirtalis, which we learned upon looking him up in a nature book. He's actually the only type of snake to be found on the Island (*so I thought at the time, although now red-bellied and green snakes are listed*) and is non-poisonous so we had nothing to fear. I had never been partial to snakes but Tham was so handsome with his three yellow-orange stripes, and he was after all, part of Shiregreene. He'd probably been there long before we began to alter his environment. We soon grew quite fond of him, checking early on sunny mornings to see him basking in the warmth on the concrete slab.

Occasionally he'd play hide and seek among the plants, only darting away if he decided we'd come too close in our search. That was likely how he'd escaped our notice for so long. Red-forked tongue reading the scents, Tham would ooze around the edge of the concrete and disappear under it through the hidden entrance to his cool, dark home. Sometimes he'd be found curled up the stalk of a dahlia, sheltered from the hot noon sun by its large leaves. We hoped Tham appreciated the changes we'd made. He must have approved, for he didn't move out.

One day a special treat awaited us. Tham was not about, but we knew he'd been there recently. He'd left behind the suit of skin he'd outgrown and shed in one complete and perfect transparent piece. Even the bulges where his eyelids had been were there. The next time Tham appeared, his coat gleamed with renewed brilliance.

Our reptilian resident must have found sufficient food around the old pump. He never seemed to stray far from it. We had seen toads in the garden, and of course there were plenty of field mice. He may have ventured farther at night when there was no curious dog to sniff at him, or vibrations of humans clumping about to startle him.

Visitors to Shiregreene were told with pride of our tenant. Their reactions were one of two types: genuine interest followed by disappointment if Tham retreated underground before he could be suitably admired, or a curious desire to view the flowerbed and pump from a considerable distance.

We like to think that Tham had accepted us, or at least was willing to tolerate our presence in his domain. Perhaps that situation contributed to his sad demise, however. We had always watched for movement near the flowerbed when we approached with the lawn tractor. Tham usually slithered in among the plants if he had been taking his leisure in the grass. It was the day after the lawn had been cut that we found Tham's body among the geraniums. He had several cuts across his richly patterned length, and we can only assume that he did not move out of the way of the machine in time.

With remorse, we buried him among the flowers of his home. His bright, black eyes, darting red tongue and lively presence were sincerely missed. And the old pump became more than just a garden centrepiece. It was now our memorial to Tham.

Fruits of Summer

Remember how summer seemed to take forever to arrive? Last fall, we watched the greens turn to gold, bronze and finally to brown. We patiently endured the bare branches of winter and rather less patiently the cool indeterminate spring. At long last, summer is in full bloom again. And we know it will pass all too quickly on Prince Edward Island.

A bustle of activity takes over the land. Time is short. In barely more than three months of "more or less" guaranteed warmth, a new generation of nature must unfold and grow strong. You can put real thoughts of winter to the back of your mind, but subconsciously the whole of summer will be spent preparing for those bleak days that are waiting in the wings.

As in many parts of Canada, planting a garden on the Island is a special challenge. With only so many days between the last and first frost, it takes planning and a measure of luck to coax the vegetables to maturity. Choosing short season varieties from the local seed house is the key. Then, one can be sure the tomatoes will just make it. There will be time to enjoy some red ones fresh off the plants. But the last green ones will have to ripen spread out on newspapers on the basement floor. Cucumbers and corn will grow plump and juicy on the plentiful showers. Those famous PEI potatoes and carrots thrive in the rich red soil. And then there are the strawberries.

The strawberry picking ritual came to symbolize summer in full swing to us, yet we never had to plant our own. There were two parts to this ceremony—if we wanted huge, perfect berries, all we needed were several containers (size, shape or original purpose not important), a pair of wellies and a bright sunny morning. A pleasant drive along picturesque country roads took us to the nearest farm that advertised "pick-your-own" by the pound. There we passed a delightful morning filling pots, buckets and baskets to the brim, visiting across the rows with other Islanders and those tourists lucky enough to discover the fun, then lining up to have the berries weighed on the scales set up in the shade at the edge of the field. A wait of any length, with the sun now high in the sky, usually ensured that some berries never made it as far as the scale. The local grocery store was never like this!

Back home, I spent the afternoon cooking batches of jam, or tucking the fragrant sun-ripened fruit into the deep freeze to preserve the flavour of this day for those months when summer itself is just a memory. It was an all-day project. The earliest pickers got the choicest spots among the dewy plants (remember the wellies?) and their baskets filled quickly. By evening, rows of carefully hand-labelled jars lined the kitchen counter and, of course, we ate fresh strawberries and cream for dessert.

The second way to celebrate strawberry season required only a small container and a sun hat. This time, we walked back to the woodlot behind Shiregreene. In among the long grass at the edge of the woods, we'd find them—tiny nuggets of red.

Small, to be sure, but wild berries have a flavour worth ten times their size. The sun would beat down as we stooped and searched with care. Soon the mound of small treasure would grow. It was worth the sunburn, mosquito bites and the aching back for just one small batch of jam or enough for one shortcake. The annual ritual was now complete. Summer could proceed.

We humans were not the only ones who would enjoy summer's nourishment later. While the farmer's black and white cows crunched their fill of juicy greens from the pasture across the road, much more was being readied for their winter meals. Toward the end of June, just before strawberry season and the really warm days set in, the crews would arrive to cut and bale the hay. The job stretched over days, even weeks if the weather turned wet. First the waist-deep grasses were trimmed off, the razor-sharp blades snipping hungrily. The entire field toppled before them like a house of cards, leaving only enough to ensure strong, new growth for a second crop.

Rabbits and mice fled as their shelters collapsed. Some hesitated too long. Soon the ravens and crows would gather for an easy meal. The sweet aroma of freshly cut grass and clover drifted in the air. Sun and summer breezes would do their part for a day or two. Gradually the grass dried and turned golden. Several times, the farmer would turn it, checking carefully for dampness.

If the good weather held, it wouldn't be long before he was back, towing behind his tractor a machine that tumbled the hay into billowy windrows ready for the baler to gobble up and spew out in tightly packed bundles. The rhythmic thump-thump of the baler had a hypnotic effect on a warm summer afternoon. Try to read, in a lawn chair in the shade of the snowball bush while they're baling hay across the road and you'll be asleep in no time!

Every day, tractors crawled along the road with over-loaded hay wagons rumbling behind. The cows hung their heads over the fence, inspecting the cargo and chewing their cuds thoughtfully. Were they dreaming of munching on those golden bales when the winter storms raged around the barn?

All through July and August the grain fields soaked up the nourishing rain and sun. a whole spectrum of colour changes occurred, from new green all the way to a rich, burnished gold. Kernels on the oats grew plump and the barley tassels rippled like silky hair as the wind stroked the fields.

GILLIAN RICHARDSON

Up and down the road, acres of potatoes covered the rolling landscape as far as the eye could see. Their deep green foliage made the land look lush and bountiful, disproving the diminutive image of the Island.

Even as the cooler nights of August gave notice that summer's lease was running out, yet another treat awaited. Wild blueberries abounded in the hedgerows around Shiregreene. We'd located the plants early in the summer, easily recognizing the tiny oval leaves. We checked their progress from time to time, impatient for the pearly white berries to ripen to deep purplish-blue. Of course, the birds took a share, but left plenty to pick for juicy pies, sweet jams and piping hot muffins to eat in front of the Franklin when snowflakes flew again.

Although we couldn't pick them yet, we knew where cranberries were ripening slowly. They'd be ready in September or early October, in full view along the roadsides in the park on the north shore, or way down where the stream resurfaced in the valley behind our place, growing in profusion among the tamaracks. We looked forward to that excursion. It was like finding an extra present under the Christmas tree when you thought they'd all been opened. By then, summer's warmth had faded, but her generosity promised her inevitable return. Our taste buds confirmed it.

Part 4: Frosty Nights and Firelight
Night Sky

Darkness lingers into the morning hours and descends again by suppertime now that summer solstice is well past. On clear nights, frost is almost a certainty. Our 6 AM excursions have given way to longer dreams and those leisurely summer evening walks through the hay fields are only memories. In their place, a run for the dog after work has to suffice, along with a short bedtime stroll around the garden to stretch our legs after several hours of sitting by the fire.

If it weren't for Toby, who demanded this late evening ritual, we may have remained ignorant of the sensuous treasure that awaited us out there. It's often missed in town, where the reflection from artificial lights spoils one's night vision. Or we simply don't look up. In the countryside, though, the sky becomes a showcase of stars. Darkness surrounds you, so the starlight draws your eyes upwards. Even peeking through the stark bare branches of the trees you can see them, a million twinkling jewels in place of summer's leaves. Everywhere you look, round the whole 360 degrees of horizon a breathtaking array of ancient patterns hangs suspended on black velvet.

If you step outside before moon rise, the stars' brilliance is magnified. Some are sharp and bright, some blend together in diffuse patches of stardust. Many seem to move, to sparkle, to dance to some secret rhythm. Try to count them? A foolish notion. It only brings on mind-boggling thoughts of infinity and makes you wonder what forever means.

We weren't devoted students of astronomy. To tell the truth, it might have spoiled the effect to analyze too much. I knew enough to recognize the Big Dipper, of course, and to locate the Pole Star from its tip. And I recalled enough from listening to my mariner father talk about navigating by the stars at sea to identify Orion, easy to spot with his spangled belt and hunting dogs at his heels. But the sheer multitude of tiny lights is overwhelming. How minute we are in all that vastness! How infinitesimal is our entire world. From one of those pinpricks of light, our blue-green Earth must appear likewise. Who might be out there looking, wondering...? How much there is that we will never....but wait...did you see it? Over there, a sudden spear of white, heading for the horizon. It lasted only a few seconds. Our neighbours had often spoken of the shooting stars they'd seen out here. Was it really there, or did we just wish it to be? (*On a visit back to the Island years later, we camped at the north shore and lay on a picnic table to take in the Perseid meteor shower on an August night.*)

At night the outdoors takes on new and intriguing qualities. The magic in the sky is just one of them. On the Island, the coming of darkness often stills the persistent wind, for a while at least. In the calm, small sounds seem to travel great distances. Apart from the occasional muffled thunder-roll of a passing jet, whisking its human cargo through the time zones, most sounds are earthbound and timeless. Across the road the crunch of frost-crisped grass under the cows' hooves startles us. A farm dog barks down the road somewhere, and faint laughter reaches our ears. On rare occasions we feel the movement of air—a nocturnal hunter glides past on silent wings. When Toby explores the tree line, the darkness swallows him up. We have to follow his progress by listening to the succession of sniffs and snorts as he probes for interesting smells and to the rustle of his feet in the long grass. I envy him his highly developed night senses, and feel impatient with him for abandoning us once he's coaxed us outdoors.

I wonder if his ears detect the dancing spectacle of light we can sometimes see to the north. It makes no sound audible to human ears; why then do we imagine music when the Aurora Borealis performs? The luminous streamers shimmer and flow, greens and yellows merging and evolving in kaleidoscopic designs. Perhaps the angels with their harps have discovered the multi-media approach and the electronic visual display is ours to enjoy.

The crisp air of an autumn night in the country holds tantalizing aromas and flavours. Tonight it tastes of woodsmoke—our Franklin has consumed a mixture of birch, poplar and old apple wood from the orchard for its evening meal and our closest neighbours warm their small house exclusively by airtight stove. The scents drift and mingle on the faint air currents. Before the hard freezes of winter set in, there's the tang of damp earth and moldering leaves to add. If it rains, all the scents become bolder.

Perhaps because our vision of earthly things is thwarted, other senses are sharpened, like those of the blind. Commonplace smells and sounds become a challenge to identify. On such occasions, I would like to trade places with the dog, sleeping out in his kennel with the stars for my ceiling, fluffy clouds for my blanket and a feast for all my senses.

Waiting for Winter

One morning, as the dog and I took a walk down the back field, we were startled when a man appeared at the edge of the neighbors' woods. He was dressed in a plaid jacket and the bright red cap told of his mission even before I noticed the gun he carried. Without seeing us in the heavier shadows close by the trees, he turned and moved cautiously along the open edge for a short distance then slipped back into the bush and was lost to view.

It had happened in an instant. He had stepped into and out of the picture so quickly, so unexpectedly, I began to doubt his existence. Silence filled the space where he had paused. There was nothing but a field of golden stubble, half-bare trees with the odd pale leaf loosening its grip and floating to the ground. The bright blue sky gave a rich bronzed glow to the earth in its autumn dress.

The dog at once dispelled my doubts. He stood at full alert, the hairs along his back bristling and a faint growl rumbling deep in his chest. If I had imagined the hunter, so had he.

We didn't often encounter anyone else down here. We had come to think of the place as our own. Even the farmer from down the road was considered part of the fantasy on those occasions when he came to plough or harvest. He belonged to the land. So it was disturbing to discover how easily the real world could encroach on our paradise. The worst of it was that I'd forgotten all about hunting season, not being interested in such pursuits.

Now, I'd have to take special care in the fields and woods where we'd come to feel secure. I'd have to keep the dog close—he looked too much like a fox when seen only in a fleeting glimpse. But I wouldn't stay away altogether. For a while, I could share this world with someone whose values I didn't agree with entirely. He had a right to be there too. He would probably only come when the weather was good and once winter's grip was firm and the walking more difficult most likely my snowshoe tracks would be the only human ones to be found.

But something had changed. A new consciousness had taken over. The surprise appearance of that hunter was a virtually undeniable sign of the coming winter. Of course I hadn't misread nature's subtle hints. I'd just let them seep into my subconscious at first, acknowledging them and filing them away for future consideration. I hadn't really been ready to accept them.

After all, wasn't it still August when the first blaze of red had flared among the maple trees across the road from our house? Too early for serious thoughts of winter. Even when the flowers had all gone to seed and the potatoes were ready to dig, the days remained pleasantly warm. Early mornings began to echo with the honking of geese threading their way in long lines from the north, but when you're busy planting bulbs your head is full of springtime images. The shorter days of September crept up so gently, it had been easy to pretend not to notice.

But when had the robins left, and the hares became so conspicuous with only a few brown smudges left in their new white coats? Had I been too busy to notice when the crickets had stilled their songs on frosty nights? Hadn't I seen the newly ploughed fields along the road to town? I must have been daydreaming as I watched the antics of a red squirrel rustling among the leaves collecting his stores, or stopped to marvel at the glorious plumage of a pheasant that stepped cautiously from a hedgerow.

The farmer was not such a romantic. His harvesting was done, his annual auction of surplus dairy cows had fattened the bank account. The last of the straw had been baled. His barn would be stuffed to overflowing with the winter food supply. "Not much room left," he chuckled as the last animals were collected from their pasture across the road. "They'll have to eat themselves a space!" It's a good thing some of us are so practical.

I did it every year. Without paying attention, I allowed myself to be carried along in a subtle drift of time. Something involuntary always made me want to hang onto the last vestiges of summer. Sometimes, in late fall there'd be a spell of short-sleeve weather again. Then I'd naively imagine there wouldn't be any winter at all.

Perhaps I needed a different kind of sign—a jolt to stir me from the complacency that tends to settle in once the challenges of the growing season have been met. This time, the sudden realization that hunting season had arrive aroused a tension, a sense of anticipation, of change. All of nature's hints were now obvious. The turn of the season was real.

To celebrate this new awareness required some act of participation—so we went cranberry picking. It was cold and wet, but it was the last chance before Thanksgiving. There had to be cranberries for sauce. They were plentiful and it was easy to fill a bag, though not so easy to avoid treading on the firm red balls so close to the ground. They popped at our every step and we nearly froze our fingers fumbling among the soggy leaves—which made it simple to turn our thoughts at last towards winter.

Soon there would be the first bright morning when the mist freezes into dazzling crystals of hoar frost on every branch and blade of grass. Once the world has turned white, dreams of Christmas, long evenings by the fire, snowshoeing, following tracks in the silent wood and all the pleasures of the new season would be welcome.

SEASONS AT SHIREGREENE

Epilogue

The time Trevor and I spent at Shiregreene was a turning point for us. Our lives were transformed by nature, the seasons, the weather in so many simple and obvious ways in this special place. Never again would we be able to feel completely at ease in a suburban lifestyle with its plastic landscaping, fences that made privacy only a sham, door-to-door intrusions and endless conveniences we'd found we didn't really need.

We had become attuned to a timeless cycle ruled by the calendar of activities in the Prince Edward Island countryside—the flights and songs of the birds, the excitement of watching the land turn green or the inevitability of falling leaves and snowflakes. We had learned to look to the little things, to understand the purpose of time, to quietly contemplate our feelings and our need for peace and solitude. The change had been gradual but would be permanent. We emerged from the experience committed to a naturalist's philosophy—to appreciate, to preserve and to protect what is our refuge and our link with all living things.

It became necessary to leave the Island, and Shiregreene, far too soon. But rather than look back sadly on what is gone, we have the pleasure of remembering what we gained by having been there. As everyone is the sum of their experiences so we are different now, and we possess a great treasure. We have a better sense of who we are, what we need and where we belong in the scheme of things. And we hope that, somewhere, we will find another Shiregreene.

SEASONS AT SHIREGREENE

GILLIAN RICHARDSON

Visit my blog

G[1]illian Richardson...naturally[2]

https://gmrichardson.wordpress.com/

For more about me and my writing:

https://books4kids.ca/authors/gillian-richardson/

If you enjoyed *Seasons at Shiregreene,* look for my children's fiction:

Ollie Buggins, Detective?, and *Take Me With You,* for ages 6-8

---

1. https://gmrichardson.wordpress.com/

2. https://gmrichardson.wordpress.com/

My collection of short stories for readers 9-12, *An Instinct for Survival,* shares dramatic moments in the lives of 10 North American animals.

About the Author

While Gillian Richardson has lived across southern Canada, time spent in the Prince Edward Island countryside kindled her passions for nature and science. They inspired this former Teacher-Librarian and writing instructor to write 20 children's books, including both fiction (novels, picture books, chapter books, short stories), and nonfiction. Bestsellers, *Kaboom! Explosions of All Kinds*, and *10 Plants That Shook the World*, won international awards. Animal characters came to life in fun ebook adventures, *Ollie Buggins, Detective?* and *Take Me With You*. A collection of short stories with nature themes became *An Instinct for Survival*. Now, casting a look back, this collection of personal essays for older readers—*Seasons at Shiregreene*—recounts the Prince Edward Island experience.

Read more at gmrichardson.wordpress.com.